Zoo Math

Zoo Sizes

Patricia Whitehouse

Heinemann Library
Chicago, Illinois

Designed by Sue Emerson/Heinemann Library and Ginkgo Creative, Inc.
Printed and bound in the U.S.A. by Lake Book

06 05 04 03 02
10 9 8 7 6 5 4 3 2 1

Library of Congress Cataloging-in-Publication Data
Whitehouse, Patricia, 1958-
    Zoo sizes / Patricia Whitehouse.
        p. cm. — (Zoo math)
Includes index.
Summary: An introduction to the concept of size featuring zoo animals.
    ISBN: 1-58810-551-2 (HC), 1-58810-759-0 (Pbk.)
    1. Size perception—Juvenile literature. 2. Size judgment—Juvenile literature.
    3. Zoo animals—Juvenile literature. [1. Size. 2. Size perception. 3. Zoo animals.] I. Title.
    BF299.S5 W48 2002
    153.7'52—dc21

                              2001004902

Acknowledgments
The author and publishers are grateful to the following for permission to reproduce copyright material:
pp. 4T.L., 16L E. R. Degginger; pp. 4B.L., 10, 12L, 13L Dwight Kuhn; pp. 4R, 7, 8, 9, 11, 12R, 22 James P. Rowan; p. 5L W. Wayne Lockwood, M.D./Corbis; p. 5R Gerry Ellis/Minden Pictures; p. 6 Jim Brandenburg/Minden Pictures; p. 13R Frans Lanting/Minden Pictures; pp. 14L, 17R A. B. Sheldon; p. 14R Claus Meyer/Minden Pictures; p. 15T Joe McDonald/Visuals Unlimited; p. 15B Marc Epstein/Visuals Unlimited; pp. 16R, 17L, 19L Norman Owen Tomalin/Bruce Coleman, Inc.; p. 18L Michael Long/Index Stock Imagery; p. 18R Byron Jorjorian; p. 19R Tui De Roy/Minden Pictures; p. 20 Lew and Marti Ligocki/Impeccable Images; p. 21 Milton H. Tierney/Visuals Unlimited.

Cover photograph by Lew and Marti Ligocki/Impeccable Images

Every effort has been made to contact copyright holders of any material reproduced in this book. Any omissions will be rectified in subsequent printings if notice is given to the publisher.

Special thanks to our advisory panel for their help in the preparation of this book:

Eileen Day, Preschool Teacher
Chicago, IL

Paula Fischer, K–1 Teacher
Indianapolis, IN

Sandra Gilbert,
Library Media Specialist
Houston, TX

Angela Leeper,
Educational Consultant
North Carolina Department
of Public Instruction
Raleigh, NC

Pam McDonald,
Reading Teacher
Winter Springs, FL

Melinda Murphy,
Library Media Specialist
Houston, TX

Helen Rosenberg, MLS
Chicago, IL

Anna Marie Varakin,
Reading Instructor
Western Maryland College

We would like to thank the Brookfield Zoo in Brookfield, Illinois, for reviewing this book for accuracy.

Some words are shown in bold, **like this.**
You can find them in the picture glossary on page 23.

Contents

What Sizes Are Zoo Animals? 4

What Are Some Big Zoo Animals? . . . 6

Which Animal Is Bigger? 8

What Are Some Small Zoo Animals? . . 10

Which Animal Is Smaller? 12

Which Animal Is Longer? 14

Which Animal Is Shorter? 16

Which Animal Is Taller? 18

How Big Are Zoo Babies? 20

How Do Zoo Babies Change? 22

Picture Glossary. 23

Note to Parents and Teachers 24

Index. 24

What Sizes Are Zoo Animals?

wallaby

elephant

gecko

Zoo animals come in many sizes.

giraffe

hippopotamus

Zoo animals are big and small.

Zoo animals are short and tall.

5

What Are Some Big Zoo Animals?

trunk

An elephant is a big zoo animal.

It has big ears and a big **trunk**.

A **hippopotamus** is a big zoo animal.

It has a big body and a big head.

Which Animal Is Bigger?

elephant

hippopotamus

Some big zoo animals are bigger than others.

The elephant is bigger than the **hippopotamus.**

rhinoceros

polar bear

The **rhinoceros** is bigger than the **polar bear**.

What Are Some Small Zoo Animals?

A **gecko** is a small zoo animal.

It has small eyes and small feet.

A **spider monkey** is a small
zoo animal.

It has a small head and a
small body.

Which Animal Is Smaller?

| gecko | spider monkey |

Some small zoo animals are smaller than others.

The **gecko** is smaller than the **spider monkey**.

penguin

puffin

A **puffin** is smaller than a penguin.

Which Animal Is Longer?

crocodile

iguana

Crocodiles have long bodies and long tails.

A crocodile is longer than an **iguana**.

python

worm snake

Snakes have long bodies.

A **python** is longer than a **worm snake**.

Which Animal Is Shorter?

wallaby

kangaroo

Wallabies have short bodies.

A wallaby is shorter than a kangaroo.

16

gorilla

chimpanzee

A **chimpanzee** is shorter than
a gorilla.

Which Animal Is Taller?

giraffe

camel

A giraffe's long neck and long legs make it tall.

A giraffe is taller than a **camel.**

ostrich

flamingo

An **ostrich** is taller than a **flamingo**.

How Big Are Zoo Babies?

Zoo babies are not as big as their mothers.

The mother giraffe is taller than her baby.

A mother **sea lion** is longer than her baby.

How Do Zoo Babies Change?

Zoo babies do not stay small.

They grow until they are as big as their parents.

Picture Glossary

camel
page 18

hippopotamus
pages 5, 7, 8

puffin
page 13

spider monkey
pages 11, 12

chimpanzee
page 17

iguana
page 14

python
page 15

trunk
page 6

crocodile
page 14

ostrich
page 19

rhinoceros
page 9

wallaby
pages 4, 16

flamingo
page 19

polar bear
page 9

sea lion
page 21

worm snake
page 15

gecko
pages 4, 10, 12

Note to Parents and Teachers

Comparing sizes of objects lays the groundwork for children to learn measurement. *Zoo Sizes* uses zoo animals to illustrate comparisons such as small and smaller, big and bigger, and so on. You can help children make these math words part of their vocabulary by making them part of your everyday talk. For example, on a walk outside, you might point out an object, such as a mailbox, and ask children to tell you if they see anything that is shorter or taller than the mailbox. Indoors, children can arrange a group of toys into pairs based on their sizes: short and tall, big and small, long and longer, and so on.

Index

camel 18

chimpanzee 17

crocodile 14

elephant 4, 6, 8

gecko. 4, 10, 12

giraffe 5, 18, 20

gorilla. 17

hippopotamus 5, 7, 8

iguana 14

kangaroo 16

ostrich 19

penguin 13

polar bear 9

puffin. 13

python 15

rhinoceros. 9

sea lion. 21

spider monkey 11, 12

wallaby. 4, 16

worm snake. 15